D1567128

SUICIDE

when it happens to someone you know

BONNIE SZUMSKI

San Diego, CA

Printed in the United States

For more information, contact:
ReferencePoint Press, Inc.
PO Box 27779
San Diego, CA 92198
www.ReferencePointPress.com

Picture Credits:
Cover: OneLineStock/Shutterstock

6: Maury Aaseng
9: aldomurillo/iStock
10: fizkes/Shutterstock
14: Rawpixel.com/Shutterstock
19: Motortion Films/Shutterstock
20: YAKOBCHUK V/Shutterstock
23: Mr.Thanathip Phatraiwat/Shutterstock
27: Stock-Asso/Shutterstock
31: Amélie Benoist Khakurel/Science Source
33: LeventeGyori/Shutterstock
36: bymuratdeniz/iStock
40: Prostock-studio/Shutterstock
42: Akarawut Lohacharoenvanich/iStock
45: Kraig Scarbinsky/iStock
48: SpeedKingz/Shutterstock
51: Inu/Shutterstock

LIBRARY OF CONGRESS CATALOGING-IN-PUBLICATION DATA

Names: Szumski, Bonnie, 1958- author.
Title: Suicide : when it happens to someone you know / by Bonnie Szumski.
Description: San Diego, CA : ReferencePoint Press, [2023] | Includes bibliographical references and index.
Identifiers: LCCN 2022021939 (print) | LCCN 2022021940 (ebook) | ISBN 9781678203542 (library binding) | ISBN 9781678203559 (ebook)
Subjects: LCSH: Suicide--Juvenile literature. | Suicide victims--Juvenile literature.
Classification: LCC HV6545 .S98 2023 (print) | LCC HV6545 (ebook) | DDC 362.28--dc23/eng/20220603
LC record available at https://lccn.loc.gov/2022021939
LC ebook record available at https://lccn.loc.gov/2022021940

contents

introduction

If Only . . .

On July 14, 2014, my son killed himself at the age of thirty-four. I thought then that I wouldn't survive his death. It was the worst thing I have ever (and hope to ever) experience. From the moment I found out, I knew that if I survived, my life would never be the same.

For my daughter and me, it seemed as though everything had been ripped away. I no longer had two children; she no longer had a brother. We clung to each other and made a vow not to harm ourselves—ever. Even though we no longer had the will to live, we knew we could not survive without one another. I had to be there for my daughter. It felt to me that she was the only thing that tethered me to the world.

Guilt, Pain, and Grief

In the beginning, in spite of people telling me that I could not have changed my son's decision, in my heart I knew it was my fault that he had taken this drastic step. Over and over, I went through everything I had said and done and everything I hadn't said and done. I berated myself many times for every fault I found in my behavior, knowing that if I had done better, he would still be here. On bad days, I still fully believe this. On good days, I know that I cannot take away my son's own volition. He was, after all, an adult. His choice, as much as I disagree with it, and as much as I believe it was made from a bout with mental illness, was still his alone.

I found I could no longer focus on daily tasks. I couldn't read. I couldn't write. I had to conserve my energy, or I would end up crying for most of the day. I couldn't sleep. I couldn't eat. I struggled to perform daily tasks. I longed to not have to get up, to not have to do the daily tasks. I just wanted my living nightmare to end.

After about three years, I stopped asking that I be allowed to die. I realized that I was willing to keep going. Though I still grieved for my son every day, I had struggled and found purpose in my life. It was not the same life I had before he died. I had changed my job. I had moved from the house he grew up in. I had begun to live an entirely different life. But it had slowly become a life. I could read again. I could focus again.

For those, like me, who have had a relative or friend die from suicide, there is no real way of reconciling the feelings of guilt—even if such feelings are completely unrealistic and unhelpful. There is a sense that if you had only done *something*—*anything*—it would not have happened, and it rings true right to the core. And yet chances are you did nothing to cause the death.

"I found I could no longer focus on daily tasks. I couldn't read. I couldn't write. I had to conserve my energy, or I would end up crying for most of the day."

—Bonnie Szumski, author

So Many Stories

Just how does one come back from the terrible feelings of guilt, loss, and suffering after a suicide? There is no one way, no magic elixir, and no ideal path back to feeling okay again. And many people face this same type of suffering each year. According to the National Center for Health Statistics (an agency of the Centers for Disease Control and Prevention), 45,979 people killed themselves in 2020, making suicide the twelfth leading cause of death in the United States for that year. When broken down by age, in 2020 suicide was the third leading cause of death for ages 10 to19; the second leading cause of death for ages 20 to 34; and the fourth leading cause of death

What the Numbers Show

Suicide is a leading cause of death in the United States. In 2020, according to the Centers for Disease Control and Prevention, 45,979 Americans died by suicide. It is the third leading cause of death for ages 10–19; the second leading cause of death for ages 20–34; and the fourth leading cause of death for ages 35–44.

Percentage of people who died by suicide and had a diagnosable mental health condition at the time of their death	90%
Percentage of US communities that did not meet federal guidelines for the number of mental health providers needed to serve residents	72%
Percentage of Americans who have been affected by suicide in some way	54%
Percentage of suicides involving firearms	53%
Percentage of Americans age 18+ living with a mental health condition who received treatment in the past year	46%
Percentage of American adults who have thought about suicide	10%

Source: American Foundation for Suicide Prevention, "Suicide Data: United States," 2020. https://afsp.org.

for ages 35 to 44. According to the same report, many more people thought about killing themselves or attempted to do so. In 2020, 10 percent of adult Americans thought about suicide, and an estimated 1.2 million Americans attempted suicide.

The effects of suicide go far beyond the individual. The National Center for Health Statistics finds that more than half of all Americans (54 percent) have, in some way, felt the effects of suicide. With these numbers, it is not surprising that so many people personally know someone who has committed suicide. For everyone who dies this way, many more grieve. There are many groups of people who meet to talk about suicide. Unlike other types of death, suicide can carry a stigma, and many who grieve find it difficult to talk to someone who has not been through it. Thankfully, many are willing to share their stories and their pathway back to leading a useful life—no matter how shattered and different that life is from before.

The many stories found in this volume are very different and very alike at the same time. In each, people admit to losing their way and finding a complicated way back. For those who go on living, purpose can slowly come back. There is no wrong or right way to do it. As the ancient Chinese proverb says, each journey begins with a single step.

chapter one

When Someone You Know Dies from Suicide: How Can It Be?

Most people are shocked when confronted by a suicide. Even if the person talked about it beforehand, it's a shock. No one expects someone they know or love to go through with it. The shock of it and the immediacy of the grief makes a suicidal death different from many other deaths people can experience.

Survivors are often left in the dark about the suicidal person's plans and ideations. Or at least that is the first reaction of most family and friends. "We were planning a family vacation and talking about high school graduation. He seemed so happy," Mike says of his son. "Now I see that he may have been trying to throw me off track so I didn't try to stop him."[1] One friend of a suicide victim says, "We had just talked and he said he wanted to give me a few of his things I had always admired. We met up and had a fun time. He was laughing and joyous. I never would have guessed."[2]

The suddenness of the death, along with the acknowledgment that the death occurred at the loved one's own hands, often multiplies the sense of loss, shock, and grief. A suicide is different from any other death. And survivors must face some of the worst discoveries of their lives as they come to terms with it.

"But there are times like now, that I wish I could pull out the note, and read it. Maybe to be reminded of what a dire state my husband was in."[4]

—Anonymous suicide widow

The Suicide Note

It's commonly thought that people who commit suicide leave behind notes. In actuality, most do not. According to the website Speaking of Suicide, only 15 to 38 percent of people who die by suicide leave a note. For the grieving, both a note and the absence of a note can be vexing, puzzling, and aggravating. But because it is the person's last words and thoughts, the grieving place dramatic importance on the note—many to the detriment of their own mental health. "I thought the note was bull****," says Mike. "He wrote that we will be much happier once he is gone. Doesn't he realize he killed all of us when he killed himself?!"[3]

No one expects someone they know or love to kill themselves. Even if the person talked about it beforehand, suicide is shocking and deeply painful for friends and loved ones who are left behind.

Others are upset when no note is present. In a blog post quoted on the Speaking of Suicide website, one woman writes:

> I have struggled off and on with the fact that my husband did not leave me a suicide note.
>
> I am once again struggling with this. I have been for weeks now. Through talking to other suicide widows, I know that the suicide note doesn't always bring comfort. It often times places blame, doesn't make any sense, or just flat out, doesn't bring ENOUGH love and affection to such a horrible situation.
>
> But there are times like now, that I wish I could pull out the note, and read it. Maybe to be reminded of what a dire state my husband was in. That death was his only option. Or just to see "I love you" one more time.[4]

Suicide notes are not all that common. When a person does leave a note, it often leads to more questions than answers. Yet, the absence of a note can have the same unsettling effect.

Even if the note is thoughtful and provides some answers, it can never take away the terrible loss. A note rarely brings satisfaction or closure to the grieving.

Complicated Emotions

Friends and family can also feel a unique sense of abandonment and betrayal upon hearing of the suicide. For some, it is hard not to take the death personally—to ask the question, why did this person do this to me? In my own experience, it created a spiritual crisis of epic proportion. How could this boy whom I raised and nurtured just leave me? Yes, I made some epic mistakes, but why couldn't he have stuck it out?

Suicide is complicated—many people don't want to talk about it. They think of it as shameful and dark. Or they want to protect the suicide victim from the opinions and feelings expressed by other people. After my son killed himself, one of the people I worked with said that it made her angry. Her husband had died after a long bout with cancer. She told me he would have given anything to have one more day of life, while my son just didn't care about the gift of life. What a despicable thing to do, she said. My son had been dead for no more than a week. After she said that, I stopped telling people what happened. I realized that people would judge my son. I know he died because he just couldn't find a way to live with his pain. I had to protect him and myself from the judgments of others.

Reliving the Violent Death

Whether or not they are the ones who find the body, friends and relatives tend to replay the scene of the suicide over and over in their minds. Sometimes this process goes on for years. Finding the body of a loved one who has committed suicide leaves vivid and devastating images in a person's mind. Jen found her son. She had been upset with him when she got home from work and found that he was not at home doing his homework as she had expected. She had an app on her phone that allowed her to track

"Don't Be Sorry"

Many people feel the need to write, journal, and speak to their loved one who died by suicide. One mother responded to her son's apologetic suicide note with a heartfelt letter reply. In part, the letter reads:

> Don't be sorry. You go to great lengths in your suicide note to apologise. . . .
>
> You don't have to apologise. You were as perfect a son as I could have hoped for. You were my hero. You were loved and adored. We shared so many perfect times. . . .
>
> That you carried a dark side that you felt you couldn't share, that the burden became so great you saw no other way out from it, is nothing to be sorry for. If anything, we failed you—the world, your family, me. We owe you an apology.
>
> Thinking about the strength it took to be you overwhelms me. Surviving that required superhuman strength. And you were just a human, a son, a brother, a friend, and the sweetest, loveliest man I'll ever know. Don't be sorry. Be at rest.

Anonymous, "A Letter to My Son . . . Who Killed Himself—and Apologised," *The Guardian* (Manchester, UK), October 6, 2018. www.theguardian.com.

his location. When she saw that it was a popular local trail, a feeling of dread came over her, and she rushed to the trailhead parking lot. She saw members of a high school cross-country team coming off the trail sobbing. She heard a distant police car siren. In her gut, she knew that she was about to find her son. She ran down the trail, where she saw people staring at a body hanging in a tree a few hundred yards away. She stopped herself from going to the site, but just barely. She will never forget what she saw. Jen says:

> I have been diagnosed with post-traumatic stress disorder (PTSD) because seeing him there was an image burned in my mind forever. Part of my mind still goes back there, saying maybe if I had rushed to him I could have given him CPR and he would be alive. But I know from eye witnesses and the police report that could never have happened. I think my grieving would be different if it wasn't for the fact that I had seen my son's death.[5]

Not being the one to find the body of a loved one who has committed suicide also leaves vivid and devastating images in a person's mind. Many visit the scene of the death. My son jumped from the Bay Bridge in San Francisco. Because the death was in such a public place, many people commuting on the bridge that day posted pictures of him standing on the bridge waiting to jump. I knew the exact location of my son's last moments. I knew I would have to stand at that spot to see the last things that he had seen. I just had to be at that spot. I had to climb up on top of the railing and feel what it would be like to face death like that. I did it early in the morning, when fewer people would see me and there would be less chance of someone calling the police. In a strange way I was comforted because I could see that it would have been peaceful up there. He would have seen the ocean, a place he loved. He would have known that his body would bear little witness to the violent way he took his life.

These ruminations on the method and time of death can be with a person for years. They may never go away. Many times they are part of the grieving process and are shared with others who have known someone who died a violent death. They become part of the memory of the individual.

A Last Painful but Necessary View

Suicide can seem utterly unreal. Often there are no clues beforehand and no explanation afterward. It usually happens in private, or at least not in front of family or friends. For some survivors, this makes the need to see the body after the fact even more important. It is part of a long, painful process of acceptance. For some, being denied that part of the process is deeply troubling.

Sometimes a police officer or the coroner or funeral director tells family members that they may not be able to see the body if there is excessive damage. These things are difficult to make sense of for the newly bereaved. Bill, whose eighteen-year-old son killed himself, says, "I couldn't believe someone else was trying to make the decision for me of whether I would view my son.

Memorial services and funerals allow friends and family members to celebrate the life of a loved one who has died. The stigma of suicide keeps some people from taking part in rituals like this that are meant to provide comfort.

I was there when he was born. I saw him through all the injuries he had had as a child. I cleaned up his vomit, his feces, and his wounds. I was damned if I wasn't going to view his body. He was my child. I loved him. I needed to see him."[6]

No one can make this decision for someone else. Depending on how the person took his or her life, the damage to the body could be too much for survivors to bear. "Either may be the right decision for an individual. But it can add to the trauma if people feel that they don't have a choice,"[7] says Jack Jordan, a clinical psychologist and coauthor of *After Suicide Loss: Coping with Your Grief*. Either choice is a difficult one. While seeing the body may add closure and confirm the reality of the death, it can also lead to added trauma.

The Stigma of Suicide

Death, for most Americans, is an uncomfortable topic, but suicide carries a stigma that does not attach to other forms of death.

Some families choose not to hold a funeral or memorial service because of this stigma. Some have difficulty talking about how their loved one died. People's idle curiosity—or sometimes even the reactions of family and friends—can lead to further hurt and isolation for people who were close to the deceased.

Deciding to not have a service to avoid facing uncomfortable questions denies family members public recognition of the death and the comfort they so need at this time. Because the victim is usually young, people's prying questions—such as "Oh that's so young. How did he/she die?"—can be especially painful. Mike and Jen vowed to make sure they told everyone who asked, even if it was idle checkout line chatter about the circumstances of their son's death. "We wanted everyone to know how common it was. That they are not immune. We wanted to tell the world that suicide is epidemic,"[8] Mike says. Yet such discussions left them exhausted and beaten down.

Melissa feared that people would judge her son, so she simply pretended he was alive. "I didn't have the energy to go through

A Son's Last Wishes

Patrick Joseph Turner, known to his family as Patty, killed himself at age sixteen. On his computer, he left behind four letters and a link to a video he had made for them. His parents shared some of their son's final thoughts, including

> the unbearable stress he felt at school and his desire for us to treat each other better. He wrote of his struggle with the pressure our community puts on our kids. . . . "So much pressure is placed on the students to do well that I couldn't do it anymore. One slip up makes a kid feel like the smallest person in the world." He felt that no credit was given to the kid who displayed great character. . . . The YouTube video . . . begins "Albert Einstein once said 'Everybody is a genius but if you judge a fish by its ability to climb a tree it will spend [its] whole life believing that it is stupid.' Do you realize how many kids relate to that fish, swimming upstream in class never finding their gifts, thinking they are stupid, believing they are useless." Patty clearly put a lot of thought into this and he did not tell anyone. The pressure got to him, and even though there were people all around him to help, he reached out to no one. His last words in one letter: MAKE CHANGES.

Contributing Writer, "Parents Write Letter About 16-Year-Old Son Committing Suicide—and What Impact That Has Had," *Orange County Register* (Anaheim, CA), January 30, 2019. www.ocregister.com.

> "I didn't have the energy to go through how he died. I would just act like he was still alive to strangers. I felt they didn't deserve to hear about my son."[9]
>
> —Melissa, who lost her son to suicide

how he died," she says. "I would just act like he was still alive to strangers. I felt they didn't deserve to hear about my son. They didn't deserve to be able to pass judgment and ask idle questions."[9] These opposing responses reveal how complicated talking about suicide remains.

Even people within the same family can have differing opinions about discussing it. Some find it so shameful that they want to keep it a family secret. "It wasn't until my son died that I found out that mental illness and suicide had happened in my grandparents' generation," says one woman who asked to remain anonymous. "My mother told me that no one would speak of it in the family."[10]

Guilt and Blame

Guilt and blame are common reactions to suicide. These emotions can lead people to shoulder responsibility that might not even be theirs. Lawrence felt this way. He felt he had failed his friend. He says:

> I told my friend's mom I should have seen he was going to kill himself. I was with him the night before when he told me a story that in retrospect was about killing yourself. He even asked if I could spend the night in a voice so pleading that if I hadn't had to get up early the next day I would have stayed. I told her I blamed myself for not reaching out, getting her number, calling her about my intuition. I still feel he would not have died if I had spent the night.[11]

This overwhelming burden of guilt permeates everyone who knew the victim. Even casual acquaintances sometimes blame themselves for the slightest infraction against the victim. The impact of suicide can never be forgotten. No matter what the circumstances, the grief and sometimes self-blame can last a lifetime.

chapter two

Searching for Answers: What Happened?

When someone dies by suicide, the people left behind search for answers as to why. They go over the death, do research, and talk to other people as they try to understand what happened—to their loved one, but also what is happening to themselves. No timetable exists for this excruciating period of questioning. This process can last weeks or months or years.

No Obvious Signs

What makes this process so difficult is that family and friends often don't know what feelings, fears, or concerns led to the decision to commit suicide. Experts suggest that 20 percent of suicide victims practice self-concealment—telling no one of their plans to kill themselves. According to a 2017 study published in the *Journal of Abnormal Child Psychology*, 55 percent of youth suicides are impulsive acts, and 55 percent have never had a previous mental health diagnosis. Brad Hunstable of Fort Worth, Texas, made a documentary film called *Almost Thirteen* about the suicide of his twelve-year-old son, Hayden. Hunstable says he saw no signs that his son was vulnerable to suicide. He believes suicide is sometimes a

To a Suicidal Person, the Act Makes Sense

Lori's dad killed himself after he became mired in debt. He told no one about the extent of the debt. In a note to his three children, he explained why he would rather die than go through bankruptcy:

> No way, no how, was I going to live the life of a deadbeat—not while living anyway. Harassment and hassle for six months, and a highly uncertain future after that is not the way I chose to live, and that, for me was the right decision. . . .
>
> [It] is important for you to understand . . . the peace and comfort I gained for myself during these many final months. I knew all along what my plan of action was to be—other than a miracle and as we all may know, there aren't any—and now . . . the time came for me to cash it in.
>
> If you anguish over how I feel at this time, don't. There's no need. I'm absolutely at peace with myself . . . not at all afraid, and surprisingly, even to me, in a very good place emotionally.

For Lori's dad, the tipping point was debt. For his family, the choice he made left them with a life of heartache.

Sol, letter to his children, May 7, 1993.

reaction to something that happens in the person's life. He says, "Impulsive suicide in youth happens because a boyfriend broke up with me . . . I got into a fight with my parents . . . a girlfriend just broke up with me . . . I'm being bullied. . . . In Hayden's case, he broke his [computer] monitor for a second time right before his birthday, in the middle of a pandemic."[12]

Likewise, Jamye Coffman of Fort Worth, Texas, lost her twenty-year-old son, Aaron, to suicide. She had talked to him less than a week before his death. They spoke freely about many things, including his plans to go to a community college. It wasn't until after his death that she found out he had been depressed after his girlfriend broke up with him. He was drinking heavily, and a friend told him to speak with his mom about it. He never did. "Obviously, he wasn't thinking straight," she says. "He was angry, upset, drunk, sad—all those things. But at the time, nobody really expected this to happen."[13]

"Obviously, he wasn't thinking straight. He was angry, upset, drunk, sad—all those things. But at the time, nobody really expected this to happen."[13]

—Jamye Coffman, who lost her son to suicide

Precipitating Factors

In the religious world, such deep feelings of hopelessness after an event such as divorce, death, illness, and other trauma is referred to as the "dark night of the soul." In the scientific world, this descent into hopelessness is called demoralization. It is prominent among people who die from suicide. Researcher Yuri Battaglia explains:

> Demoralization is a syndrome clinically separated from depression. It is characterized by a combination of distress and subjective incompetence; the loss of meaning and purpose in life; the lack of perceived social support; a sense of being trapped and personal failure; a cognitive attitude of pessimism, and hopelessness/helplessness. Moreover, this psychological state has a significant role in negatively influencing . . . quality of life, coping styles, and dignity.[14]

For most people, such critical moments eventually pass. But for those who take their lives, such a crisis feels impossible to survive in the moment. They just want the pain to end.

Research suggests that youth suicides are often impulsive acts. The triggers tend to be dramatic events in the young person's life, such as a breakup between a boyfriend and girlfriend.

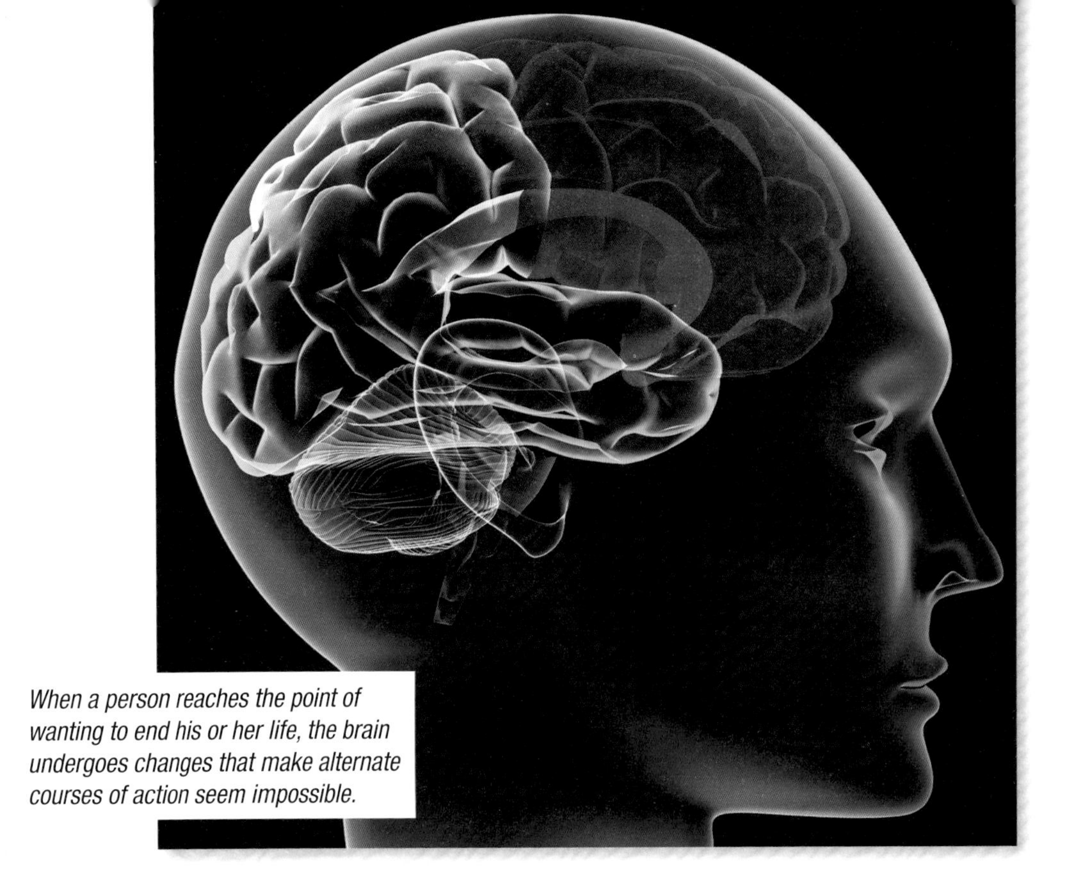

When a person reaches the point of wanting to end his or her life, the brain undergoes changes that make alternate courses of action seem impossible.

Those who have survived a suicide attempt often recall these feelings. Nancy Nettles had experienced divorce, homelessness, and a diagnosis of multiple sclerosis—all within a very short period of time. She had reached a turning point. "I remember thinking that my kids would be better off if I wasn't here. . . . I was homeless, jobless . . . I felt like someone else would be able to take care of them,"[15] Nettles recalls. She tried to kill herself with an overdose three times. Each time, she was taken to the hospital—and survived.

Physicians label this tipping point of going from surviving setbacks to suicidal ideation "cognitive constriction." Christine Moutier, chief medical officer of the American Foundation for Suicide Prevention, explains, "The actual physiological functioning of certain parts of the brain changes in this acute suicidal moment. What's happening in the brain is there's a narrowing of coping options that stems from changes in the brain's ability to come up with three or four ideas to problem-solve, like it usually would. The actual functioning of the brain changes in this acute suicidal moment."[16]

Why Did He/She Do This to Me?

These explanations of what happens when someone is in the moment of suicide can be one way of processing the question, "Why did this person do this to me?" This question often surfaces as part of processing the grief after suicide. Counselor Sam Fiorella explains:

> What I've discovered from speaking to many teens and young adults who are suffering with depression is that at their lowest moments, they are not thinking of you—or anyone for that matter. They simply can't think or experience any reality beyond the pain and anxiety they are feeling at that moment.
>
> A student suffering from depression recently said, in response to the adage that suicide is a permanent solution to a temporary problem: "You don't get it, depression ISN'T a temporary problem! It's a permanent problem."
>
> The point is, when their illness takes over, it's like any physical illness that we seem to be able to reconcile. They simply don't have the option out, just like they don't have the option out when they're involved in a fatal car crash or when an embolism explodes in their brains.[17]

Suicide attempt survivors often describe this as "I couldn't take the pain anymore" or "I saw no other way out." Physicians say that if such people are distracted sometimes for as little as ten to fifteen minutes, they can change their minds. As Moutier explains, "It's a short period when for a few minutes, maybe up to an hour, that cognitive constriction occurs . . . and that transient nature of the physical change is why if

> "What I've discovered from speaking to many teens and young adults who are suffering with depression is that at their lowest moments, they are not thinking of you—or anyone for that matter. They simply can't think or experience any reality beyond the pain and anxiety they are feeling at that moment."[17]
>
> —Sam Fiorella, counselor

Reasons Why

In a pamphlet for the American Association of Suicidology, Jeffrey Jackson lists several reasons why people kill themselves:

- Emotional illness. Up to 70% of people who die by suicide may suffer from what psychiatrists call an "affective illness" such as major depression or a bipolar disorder.
- Prior attempts. Often disguised as reckless behavior, many suicide victims have a history of prior attempts.
- Morbid thoughts. Many suicidal people are unusually comfortable with the idea of death, or convinced that a dark fate awaits them.
- Hypersensitivity to pain. Suicidal individuals often exhibit disproportionate emotional reactions to problems and hardships—sometimes even to the hardships of others. Some go to great lengths to help others because they simply cannot bear the idea of pain, even if it is not their own.
- A chronic need for control. Many people who go on to die by suicide exhibit an obsessive need for control. . . . Their natural inability to cope with pain and misfortune compels them to try to prevent it by orchestrating the events in their world to an extreme degree.

Jeffrey Jackson, *SOS: A Handbook for Survivors of Suicide*. Washington, DC: American Association for Suicidology, 2003. https://suicidology.org.

people can live through it, they can regain their usual healthy coping functions and survive long beyond that moment."[18]

Mental Illness: A Primary Cause

Some suicides are telegraphed in advance, and yet even with these warnings may not be prevented. My son had a short, undiagnosed, devastating bout with mental illness that I think precipitated his suicide. My daughter telephoned me saying my son had shown up at her apartment in a raving state. He was making no sense, paranoid about people being after him, and warning her not to eat certain foods and not to have contact with others. I got on a plane and flew out immediately. I convinced him he could trust me, and tried to calm him down. The weird thing is, he could point to real things that had happened to him that could be viewed as people following him. But to someone not experiencing what he was experiencing, I realized he was having a mental break with reality.

After taking him to an emergency room and to several doctors who prescribed rest and good food, all of which I provided, my son's condition seemed to improve. He was living with me during the crisis but wanted to go home. We made an agreement: he would see a therapist, we would talk every day, and I would visit him the following week. He decided to kill himself three days after he returned home.

Even with proper psychiatric care, there is no guarantee of a different outcome. Doris A. Fuller's daughter Natalie killed herself after fighting psychosis for six years. Her story reveals how difficult it is to get help and to maintain health. Natalie first experienced a psychotic break at twenty-two. Such breaks usually occur between the ages of eighteen and twenty-five. Natalie's stories of friends talking about her behind her back and of strange happenings didn't sound irrational enough for her mother's alarm bells to go off.

Although proper psychiatric care and medication can help people with mental illness, there is no guarantee that these interventions will stop a person from taking his or her own life.

"My daughter lived more than six years with an incurable disease that filled her head with devils that literally hounded her to death, and she did it while laughing, painting, writing poetry, advocating and bringing joy to the people around her."[19]

—Doris A. Fuller, whose daughter died by suicide

Natalie maintained that she was fine. When police officers were called after she created a public scene, they took her to a hospital emergency room, where she was diagnosed with severe bipolar disorder (in addition to psychosis). With proper medication, two months later she was stable and healthy.

Unfortunately, it didn't last. Like many people suffering from mental illness, Natalie went off her meds, which brought on more severe psychotic symptoms. She ended up spending almost a year in a psychiatric hospital. Again, she recovered. Again, it didn't last. She began to believe her disease was incurable. She still would hear voices. She decided to go off her meds for good. At age twenty-eight, Natalie took her own life. Her mother says:

> My daughter lived more than six years with an incurable disease that filled her head with devils that literally hounded her to death, and she did it while laughing, painting, writing poetry, advocating and bringing joy to the people around her. She was the bravest person I have ever known, and her suicide doesn't change that. My daughter, who lost her battle with mental illness, is still the bravest person I know.[19]

My son and Fuller's daughter are not exceptions to the rule. According to the National Alliance on Mental Illness, 46 percent of people who die by suicide had a known mental illness. The percentage of people experiencing mental illness at the time of suicide is probably higher, since many are undiagnosed at the time of their death.

Knowing the factors that led to a suicide is helpful to some, less helpful to others. Either way, the grief experienced by those who survive is not alleviated and never completely goes away.

chapter three

Survivors in the Aftermath of Suicide: What Is Happening to Me?

Bereavement is unique and complicated. Many people who have lost someone to suicide describe it as the worst pain they have ever experienced. Each person grieves differently, and there is no one way to grieve. In many cases, however, suicide leads to extended periods of questioning and self-examination.

A Traumatic Death

Many who grieve a suicide have similar reactions to those who have experienced traumatic deaths as a result of homicides, car accidents, and natural disasters. Symptoms of post-traumatic stress disorder are not uncommon. These symptoms include reliving the death over and over, avoiding reminders that trigger thinking about the death, as well as physiological symptoms such as panic attacks, hyperventilation, and not being able to sleep or eat. As happens with other traumas, a griever's life is inexorably changed by the death. Life no longer can be presumed safe and predictable.

A Sister's Grief

"When I lost my brother a part of me went with him and I have tried to take my own life too as I had no one to talk to about it as I was asking why did he have to go away but got no answer. But I know he is with me always and forever. I have tried to take my own life several times but was talked out of it, and now I know my brother wants me to be strong for our mum as he was the most strong, loved man you could ever meet. As my brother once said to me when we were kids, you can be strong and love ya Sissy, always be happy and tell your family you love them. He would always smile and always loved life and family. There is a lot of pain inside of me and so very angry and this will last a life time. The pain will always remain."

—Sharon, whose brother committed suicide

Quoted in White Wreath Association, "Personal Suicide Stories," 2021. www.whitewreath.org.au.

There is a sense that if someone who is known and loved can decide to kill himself or herself, nothing in life can be taken for granted. Grievers may also feel that because they could not keep the suicidal victim from harm and did not know that it was going to happen, they cannot reasonably keep others from similar harm. Some psychologists call this *traumatic grief*.

"[Traumatic grief is] a sense-losing event — a free fall into a chasm of despair."[20]

—Glenda Dickonson, counselor

Glenda Dickonson, a licensed clinical professional counselor in Maryland, describes traumatic grief as "a sense-losing event—a free fall into a chasm of despair." She further explains that a suicidal death may cause survivors to experience a steep decline in well-being. "They are down there swirling," she says, "experiencing all the issues that are part of grief—shock, disbelief, bewilderment."[20]

Shock often causes people to feel frozen and unable to perform routine tasks. They may feel that they are living in a fog where nothing makes sense. Grievers can experience illness, exhaustion, and uncontrollable crying. They may feel unable to leave their homes.

Reliving the Death

Three-quarters of suicides take place in the person's home, and 23 percent of those deaths are witnessed by at least one family member. Grieving a suicide can be complicated by witnessing the death or the aftermath of the death. People who are eyewitnesses to the suicide or even those who have heard details of the death can relive the death in their minds repeatedly. "It was impossible for me to forget the way my friend died," says Scott. "He was the first one to jump off the new Bay Bridge in San Francisco. I initially thought that he probably just wanted to make it in some macabre records book. I later couldn't get it out of my mind every time I crossed the bridge."[21]

Jen, who found her son's body hanging in a tree, would also obsessively relive the memory with the thought that if she had been there even thirty minutes earlier, his suicide would not have happened. Her anxiety extended to Halloween, when some people put up a dummy hanging from a tree, which instantly brought her back to the moment of her son's death. "I eventually had to seek out a particular therapy called EMDR (Eye Movement Desensitization and Reprocessing) therapy, which helped me. At least now my triggers have been lessened and I am not continuously worried that the images will overwhelm me at any moment."[22] Jen's traumatic memories were triggered by many things and resulted in her becoming fearful and self-protective.

Grief over a suicide can result in symptoms associated with post-traumatic stress disorder. These symptoms include reliving the death over and over, panic attacks, and inability to sleep or eat.

A Loss of Predictability and Safety

Many grievers experience feelings of loss of identity, loss of control, and loss of all assumptions. In my experience, I felt like the worst mother in the world. The one task of parents is to keep their child alive. I had failed at that. My whole life was shattered. I would feel panicked and stuck if I ran to the market and had an idle conversation. Some stranger asking "How many children do you have?" would send me into paroxysms of loss of identity and self-worth. I mistrusted myself completely. I used to offer tidbits from personal experience when people asked for my advice. After my son's death, I stopped. How could I ever offer advice again? I, who couldn't keep my son alive? This sense of mistrust of one's own instincts and that life happens in a fairly predictable, controllable way is shattered. A new, frightening reality, that a terrible event can rip these assumptions away, is typical of traumatic grief.

Unique Grief from Unique Circumstances

Although people who grieve a suicidal death share some things with all people who grieve, one of the things that sets a suicidal death apart from other deaths is knowing that the deceased made a choice to end his or her life. While some psychologists argue that even this assumption should be challenged, since most

A Stranger's Kindness

"I found out that my dad committed suicide [when I was shopping] at Hobby Lobby. . . . The woman who consoled me was 8 months pregnant, and up until that moment, she was nervous and excited about motherhood. Without a moment's hesitation, she was on the ground, stroking my back, and helping me off the floor, called my boyfriend at the time and told my managers. My world had just ended, and so effortlessly, she began to make some sense of it. In that moment, I think she knew she'd make a great mom. Without really knowing me or anything other than my dad had just committed suicide, she knew to be present. I often wonder where she is and what she's doing in the world and what her family looks like . . . but I know I'll always be grateful for her being there when I lost mine."

—Ashley Wiersma, whose father killed himself

Quoted in Colby Itkowitz, "Telling Their Heartbreaking Stories About Suicide Loss Started a Powerful Conversation," *Washington Post*, March 31, 2016. www.washingtonpost.com.

people who kill themselves are experiencing a mental health crisis, grievers are pained by the thought that their loved one chose to leave them. Psychologist John R. Jordan explains the ramification of this belief:

> Whenever a mourner believes that someone intended a death to happen, this belief seems likely to add an extra layer of guilt and rage to the emotional response to the death. To the degree that a suicide death is also perceived as intended, then, it raises profound meaning-making and existential questions for the mourner. Why would they choose to do this? How could they have overcome their fear of death, their responsibilities, and their love for others to engage in this behavior? If this death was chosen, then could the deceased, or myself, or someone else have prevented that choice? Why wasn't my relationship with the person enough reason to stay alive? Whose "fault" was the death, and who should be held accountable for it? To a greater or lesser degree, these are the questions with which most suicide loss survivors wrestle. They are also questions that often do not have simple or socially consensual answers, which can create a high level of angst on the part of many survivors.[23]

Jordan's explanation rings true for many grievers. Survivors experience a prolonged period of questioning that can cut to the very heart of what it means to be alive. Jenny Teo describes the unfathomable sense of loss she experienced after her son Josh killed himself.

> Guilt and condemnation can quickly take over every cell in your body and make you want to end it all too. It also dawned on me that with him gone, I had lost the only link I had to my future. A future which I had built my entire life upon when I made the decision to quit my career, to start

a family, and be a homemaker at the age of 37. How can I turn back time and start all over again? Losing Josh was losing my only chance of ever becoming a grandmother—not to mention great-grandmother plus a whole generation after him.[24]

Along with questions of how someone could intentionally decide to give up on life come questions about who is responsible for the death. Family and friends often blame themselves. Marilyn experienced this after her friend killed himself. She says,

> You know I really blame myself for my friend's death. He started working at a job that required him to be there at all hours. After inviting him out a few times and him saying no, I gave up on him and stopped calling. Then I heard from his mother that he had killed himself. I knew he had dark periods of loneliness. And yet I just forgot to call. Really, I would think, what was more important than your friend's life![25]

Others go through painful feelings of having to acknowledge that they may not have known their loved one very well. According to clinical psychologist Richard Tedeschi, parents can be especially tormented by these thoughts: "If your child seemed to be thriving and there were no warning signs, you think you should have noticed them. If you knew your child was struggling, you feel you should have been more vigilant to prevent the suicide."[26]

> **"I had to understand that my daughter was in so much pain that she would feel no one and nothing could make life worth living."[24]**
>
> —Julie Halpert, whose daughter died from suicide

In addition to disconnectedness, there are feelings of betrayal and sadness around the fact that the person did not give friends and family members a chance to intervene. "My friend knew I was a therapist," says Marilyn. "We had talked so many

A patient undergoes hypnosis during an EMDR therapy session. When traumatic memories are triggered, techniques learned through therapy can prevent those memories from becoming overwhelming.

times about so many issues. I was shocked when I learned he didn't trust me enough to tell me about how he was feeling. I felt betrayed. But I also felt sad. Why wasn't I a good enough friend to understand he needed me?"[27]

Blaming Others

Grievers may also go through periods of intense anger and blame others for the death. I took my son to an emergency room, but while my son confessed that he was hearing voices and felt that someone was out to get him, he denied that he wanted to end his life. After my son explained that he had been working really long hours, the doctor thought he was experiencing symptoms from overexertion and exhaustion. My son killed himself two weeks later. I later learned that I could have demanded a psychological evaluation. I was so angry at that doctor. He was a trained professional. I was just a mom.

Lori's father was being hounded by creditors and didn't know how he would get out from underneath the crushing debt. He

"You know I relished telling every one of those creditors about my dad's death. He was beyond their hounding now."[28]

—Lori, whose father died by suicide

signed a pact with his three children that he would not kill himself. He later rented a hotel room and shot himself. Lori says, "You know I relished telling every one of those creditors about my dad's death. He was beyond their hounding now. I blamed them in part for his decision to kill himself."[28] While it would seem obvious to blame the person who killed himself or herself, few grievers blame the deceased for the death.

Restoring a Will to Live: Controlling Grief and Thoughts of Self-Harm

Grieving from any loss is difficult and involves an intense longing for the deceased. But psychologists agree that there is an uptick in thoughts of ending one's own life after a loved one's suicide. Survivors may want to actively kill themselves or simply hope that an accident will end their pain. According to the website Psychiatry Advisor, a study of 3,432 young adults who had lost close friends or family members to suicide found that they had a higher probability of attempting suicide than individuals bereaved by sudden deaths due to natural causes. Mike recalls:

> A couple weeks after my son's death I grabbed a six pack of beer (I had given up drinking years before) and headed up a two-lane road fully intending to launch myself off the road. I couldn't deal with the pain. I didn't want to live another day of it. As I was driving down this highway, I realized how much grief I would cause my wife and daughter. I knew they could not survive. I took the six pack, dumped it, and began the drive home and the slog of continuing to live out the pain.[29]

Overwhelming feelings of self-blame and unbearable guilt can lead people to engage in risky behavior. As Mike says, "I remem-

Needing to blunt the pain and guilt of suicide loss, people sometimes engage in risky behavior—like walking along railroad tracks or driving without a seatbelt—that could lead to their own death. These thoughts usually subside with time.

ber vividly when I decided to no longer wear my seat belt. If a car accident happened, I thought, I might get lucky."[30] Others report intentionally walking along dangerous roads or along railroad tracks lost in thoughts of ending their lives to end the pain.

Thankfully, most suicidal ideation after a suicidal death subsides with time. For those who continue to have such thoughts, seeking out the help of a psychologist or medical doctor can help. The whirlpool of despair that comes from the death of a loved one can overwhelm anyone, but in the case of a suicide, the effects may continue for a lifetime.

chapter four

How to Talk to Someone Who Has Experienced a Loss from Suicide

As hard as it is to imagine, sometimes the deepest pain comes not from the suicide but from how people react to it. I remember that my sister had never understood my son. My son had always gone his own way and put an emphasis on fun in his life. Consequently, I was always helping him out of fixes, and he was never financially a success. After he killed himself, my sister said, "At least you don't have to worry about him anymore." Because she was the one I had relied on in those first days, this came as a particularly hard blow. To this day I don't know whether she understood how hurtful this comment was.

The Stigma of Suicide Can Create Further Loss

Despite many efforts over many years to increase public awareness and understanding of suicide, it still bears a stigma of shame. That stigma can lead to insensitive remarks. The stigma can also cause people to avoid any discussion of what has happened and why. Experts say that refusing to talk about the person who has committed suicide is unhealthy. It can also tear a family apart. Jill's brother killed himself by overdose in his room while the whole family was home. When his body was found, the siblings reacted with shock and grief, but her parents said very little, and the children were given the impression they should not talk about it. "My mother and father just had no way to cope with or talk about his death," Jill says. "They were always uncomfortable talking about feelings. I sought out my best friend and an older friend to talk to. Even today, if I want to talk about the circumstances of my brother's death, my mother and sister are abrupt with me. They have said that they think I should be over it by now."[31]

> **"People really, really don't like you saying suicide. . . . It makes other people uncomfortable I think. . . . I think it's a lot easier to have a conversation with someone about the death of their grandma."[32]**
>
> —Young woman who lost a friend to suicide

Suicide stigma can be so obvious to the grieved that they stop mentioning the word *suicide* in relation to the death of the person. One young woman whose friend killed himself says, "People really, really don't like you saying *suicide*. . . . It makes other people uncomfortable I think. . . . I think it's a lot easier to have a conversation with someone about the death of their grandma, who's . . . passed away in her sleep, or whatever, I think, because it's just less of an awkward topic . . . and you don't have to try and think about someone's intentions."[32]

Rushing Does Not Help

Because the death is sudden and a survivor is often unable to cope with the necessary tasks of the death, mourners may be reliant on family and friends to help with those tasks. How those tasks are completed can also leave lasting scars. Family members and others may rush mourners to get over the death, quickly trying to remove physical memories of the person in a mistaken effort to help. A thirty-three-year-old woman whose partner had died by suicide nine years prior to her interview said, "After my

The urge to take away the pain of suicide loss can be strong. But rushing to clean out a room or remove memories of the person who has died can cause more harm than good for the person who is grieving the loss.

partner passed I was treated different, not wanting me to talk about it, all traces gone from families' houses and our house cleared out. But I think that was what my family thought I wanted, but I didn't. I realise now I could not and will not be able to talk to family about my issues again."[33]

Mara, who was in her thirties when her brother killed himself, recalled a similar situation. She explains:

> The final time I went to my brother's apartment was difficult. My aunt and my boyfriend were there and seemed in a hurry to clean out the space and leave. Everything felt rushed. If it had been my mom and me alone, we would have stayed longer. I wanted to be in my brother's space, with his things, and feel close to him. When my mom and me went to my brother's apartment, my aunt and boyfriend went along. They were in a hurry to clean up the space and leave. My mom tried to do what they wanted and everything felt rushed. I knew if it had just been my mom and I we would have stayed longer, I wanted to be in my brother's space, with his things, and feel close to him.[34]

It is hard for family and friends to see grievers so helpless, and the urge to take away some of the pain by taking care of things like cleaning out a room can seem a concrete way to help them. It is difficult to wait out the confusion to find the right actions.

Idle Curiosity

When survivors of a suicide death go back to work or rejoin their circle of friends, the curiosity of others can be difficult to bear. Some of the most hurtful responses are prying questions, some of which come across as veiled blame. "People are searching for answers so they can feel immune to it happening to them," Jen says. "Friends would ask, 'Weren't there signs? Was your family close?' without even realizing how painful these questions are. Having to defend our family after such a traumatic event added to our pain and isolation."[35]

> "Having to defend our family after such a traumatic event added to our pain and isolation."[35]
>
> —Jen, who lost a son to suicide

Such curiosity can also feel like the questioners are trying to prove to themselves it could not happen to their family. While it is natural for people to try to seek answers to reassure themselves that their son, daughter, or family member could not die by suicide, these types of questions can further isolate the bereaved. Melissa says, "I wanted to shout, YOU ARE NOT IMMUNE! When people asked questions that were clearly meant to pinpoint issues so that they could say, ah, that's it, that's why it can't happen to me."[36]

False Empathy

In the face of terrible tragedies, it is natural for people to offer reassurance. Telling a person who has lost someone to suicide that you understand how they feel and what they're going through can be a tremendous comfort coming from someone who has actually experienced suicide. On the other hand, it can be upsetting when

Hurtful Comments

When they had been divorced just a year, Susan lost her ex-husband to suicide in 2005. Part of her advice to others is to know that

> sometime, someone somewhere is going to say something that will devastate you. Some of the things that were said to me were, "God has a plan,"—I mean, a plan to take my ex-husband's life? or someone told me: "It was part of his past life. He had to get on to the next life." You will remember some of these comments for years, and they are like a stab in the heart. They will happen. Be prepared.

Susan, interview with the author, April 6, 2022.

someone seeks to offer reassurance by comparing the feelings associated with death by suicide to other deaths. Gayle Brandeis, in an article for the *New York Times*, recalls:

> A few days after my mother took her life in 2009, my husband shuttled me and our newborn to our first postpartum/postnatal checkup. I was still reeling from the news of my mom's suicide; she had died when the baby was 1 week old. I wasn't sleeping; I could barely speak; it was hard to convince myself to leave the house for the checkup—every nerve in my body was on edge, braced for the next disaster.
>
> Our midwife's assistant led us to the cozy exam room in our midwife's home, and offered me a glider chair. I couldn't keep the tears at bay as I sat down; I leaked tears and milk as I slid the chair back and forth, clutching the baby to my breast for dear life. The assistant sighed and said "I know just how you feel. My ex had a heart attack last week."
>
> She hadn't talked to him in years, she said. . . .
>
> "You don't know how I feel; you don't know how I feel," I started chanting in my head. By the time the midwife entered the room, I was inconsolable.[37]

Religious Responses to a Suicide Mourner

While religious or spiritual guidance helps some, for others it offers no comfort or, worse, adds to the pain. Platitudes meant to comfort (such as "He's in a better place" or "God needed her more than you did") can be especially difficult to hear.

Pastor Mary Robin Craig explains that suicide survivors need support and compassion, not simplistic statements that suggest there is a good side to what has taken place. She explains:

> Praying with someone about loss from suicide is not the time for casual platitudes about God's plan or God's supposed need for another angel in heaven. It is most especially not a time to try to tell a survivor—someone who has lived through a loved one's death by suicide—those often misquoted words, "God never gives us more than we can handle" (erroneously based on 1 Corinthians 10:13, which specifically addresses temptation to sin, not endurance of grief). To say in these circumstances that God is implicated in some sort of test of one's capacity for managing traumatic experiences may result in the suicide survivor's further dismay and alienation from God. Neither is it the time to say, "I know how you feel," since (unless you yourself are a survivor) you do not know, nor to say, "I can't imagine." The latter comment establishes a barrier between you and someone who already feels isolated from others, and it conveys a sense that what has happened is so awful that you cannot bear to enter into the experience even as a companion.[38]

Another particularly painful response can be to suggest that the suicidal person is being punished in the afterlife for his or her decision. Jen says, "My friend kept asking if she could ask me a question. I just knew she wanted to ask me

"Praying with someone about loss from suicide is not the time for casual platitudes about God's plan or God's supposed need for another angel in heaven."[38]

—Mary Robin Craig, pastor

The best way to help a friend or family member who experiences a suicide death is to be a good listener. That means allowing the person to freely express his or her feelings about the loss.

if I thought my son was in heaven, so I kept telling her no don't ask it. She went ahead and not only asked it but offered her opinion that my son was no doubt in hell and she prayed for him every day. That was so painful."[39]

Ways to Help

Fortunately for those who wish to help a friend or family member who experiences a suicide death, it can be done. Experts say the best way to help is to listen rather than feel an immediate need to offer condolences or offer comparisons. The Counseling and Mental Health Center at the University of Texas at Austin, suggests:

> Be an active listener. Though it can be difficult to know what to say to your friend, being able to listen effectively is most important. Often finding the right words is less important than letting your friend express him/herself and share with you the nature of the loss. It's not unusual for well-meaning

> people to avoid talking about suicide or mentioning the deceased person, thinking this is helping. However, the grieving person often needs to feel that others are willing to acknowledge the truth of the situation.[40]

It's natural to want to take away someone else's pain or help the person overcome his or her pain, but it's important to understand that this isn't possible. Instead, the best and most helpful response is deep listening. That means listening to the person's complex feelings about the death without offering suggestions or making an effort to fix the person's pain. Listen to the self-blame, confusion, and anger. Be a safe place for that person to vent all the feelings without judgment. And if you cannot do that, don't pretend that you can.

Acknowledge the suicide and do not shy away from the complexities of such a death. The survivor needs to know that you will not shrink from the topic and can handle talking about death. If you did not know the suicide victim, you can ask the survivor to talk about the person and tell you about him or her. If you did

The Kindness of Others

Nadine Murray recounted many good and bad things that people said and did after the death of her daughter by suicide. Below are some of the good memories:

> Fortunately, most people are not cruel. They go out of their way to try to heal another's pain. My oldest daughter called every day to make sure I was all right. My best friend called every night and listened to me cry for hours so I could finally fall asleep.
>
> My other sister showed up frequently to fill up the fridge and cabinets, even though she lived 10 hours away. My neighbor, my friend for years, made sure that my lawn was mowed and the trees and bushes were cared for. For years, I didn't even notice. Then I did.
>
> After more than a decade, now I notice. The kindness that others have shown me has helped me to forgive myself. Forgiving myself is a wonderful thing. It's brought me back to life.

Nadine Murray, "What I Wish You Knew About Teen Suicide, from a Heartbroken Mom," *Today*, July 13, 2017. www.today.com.

know the person, share stories about him or her, and be willing to open up about why you were friends. My son's friends continue to be a comfort for me, even years after his death. When they reach out to ask how I am or tell me a small anecdote about my son, it truly brings me joy.

Offer Help Without Expecting Anything in Return

You can offer any or all help that you think will be of use, but curb your expectations that the suicide mourner is ready. Try not to feel slighted by the mourner's lack of response. Don't take it personally. While offering a food train with friends may help, suicide survivors often don't want to eat or can only eat very small amounts of food. The offered food can become as much a burden as a help. Remember to ask, "Can I help with food preparation? What are some of the things you might feel like eating?" Gift cards to local takeout places can offer variety and take away the pressure to eat others' food before it goes bad.

Offering concrete help, whether in the form of a short visit or walking the dog, can help the grieving person get through a time when he or she has little energy for any of the normal routines of daily life.

Offer concrete things such as a coming over for a visit, going for a walk, or walking the dog. Put yourself in the place of someone who has received a shock, has little energy to do anything, and may need time to sit quietly. Offer concrete help but remember that even a visit can become burdensome if it lasts too long. Check in frequently but simply to say a few words, maybe even a memory of the loved one. Don't expect a response to phone calls or texts. Remember that it isn't about you. It's about offering support without burdening the mourner.

Acknowledge Special Days

To the bereaved, every day is painful. But anniversaries can be particularly agonizing. Birthdays, the day the person died, and holidays hold special significance and pain for the bereaved. Remember to reach out on or near these days. Even a text to say you are thinking of the bereaved person can allow him or her to share memories and feelings. Remember that the pain will never go away, though it will become less a matter of dire urgency. Far from wanting to forget these days, for most mourners acknowledging special days can be a supportive way of helping the friend.

There is at least one other way to help someone who is grieving a suicide: say the deceased person's name. When you recall a story worth telling, use his or her name in that story. If you have a photo to share, talk about him or her by name. People who hurt from a suicide will never forget. It is never inappropriate to remember the person who died.

chapter five

Coming Out the Other Side: Moving from Survival to Living Again

There is no timetable for getting over grief. For survivors of a suicide death, the timetable can be even more unpredictable and long-lasting than for some other deaths. If the death was that of a family member, the entire family may go through a rearrangement of roles and have difficulties that will persist for a lifetime. If it was a close friend, there may be long-time adjustments that are made and fears that persist. For all, adjustments will be made.

A Suicide in the Family

Suicide can bring on lasting rifts in families or exaggerate the ones that were already there. In addition, families must reorganize and reconfigure themselves after the suicide. The loss of a parent means that the burden of the family now rests on one parent, who is also deeply grieving. After Andrea's father killed himself, she recalls, "my mom really couldn't be available for my sister and me. My grandmother was also grieving, but managed to take care of us most of the time. My mother did her best to keep the conversation open and answer our questions, but I also knew I should try to spare her from talking about our dad."[41]

The suicide of a brother or sister often means that the children who are left often feel a void and must seek out others for help. Mara says, "My brother was the one I always turned to when I needed to talk about the family dysfunction. He was there the day I was born. We confided in each other throughout our lives. I felt lost and untethered. I felt I had let him down. I had many regrets."[42]

Parents may also begin to create a new narrative around the child's death. They may begin to idealize the child to the point that the surviving children rebel and fight back. "I found a note that read, 'I love you mom,' clearly from when my kids were little and I started thinking about my son. My daughter piped up, 'No mom its actually your kid who didn't kill [herself] that wrote that.' It was brutal, but necessary. She needs to express her feelings about my tendency to idealize my son."[43]

Roles and relationships sometimes change after a suicide. A grandparent, who might also be grieving, sometimes has to step in to help care for children when a parent is emotionally unavailable.

Some families experience further disruption from parents not being able to make the marriage work after their child's suicide. Couples may grieve in different ways and may not be able to understand or respect each other's grief. I remember when I went to a suicide support group, a woman there told me that she didn't think her marriage would survive because her husband refused to talk about their child or about his own grief. They had no other children, and she felt very alone in her grief.

Creating a Narrative

Clinical psychologist John R. Jordan writes about several levels of "reintegration" that must occur when a family member dies by suicide. Reintegration involves creating a narrative of the death. That narrative allows for a reasonable explanation of why it happened as well as who bears responsibility for the suicide. This process is important because family members often feel shame, guilt, or that they could have (or should have) done more to prevent the suicide. As Jordan explains:

> One of the most important healing tasks for suicide loss survivors is to develop a "bearable" narrative of the suicide, one that works well enough for the survivor that they can obtain some relief from the "Why?" questions and restore a sense of coherence to their assumptive world. This usually includes construction of a narrative of the death that embraces the complexity of suicide as a kind of "perfect storm" of factors coming together (including the intentions of the deceased) that allowed the suicide to happen, rather than just the simple result of one person's mistakes or failures.
>
> This ideally includes a realistic and fair explanation of what happened, why it happened, and what responsibility the survivor should realistically and fairly assume for the event. Note that this does not mean that all people in a family must agree on all aspects of the story of what happened,

or why it happened. Rather, each family member (or person in the social network affected by the death) must develop an explanation of the death that works well enough for them psychologically, and that allows them to begin to reinvest in their life without the deceased. . . . This task also includes accepting the "blind spots" that are common after suicide, such as the fact that the only person who could answer these "Why?" questions is now dead, and unavailable to offer clarification of their behavior.[44]

Alongside this narrative, the grieving may also begin to reconfigure their relationship with the deceased person and who they were. Many survivors begin to integrate a new biography of their loved one that goes beyond the circumstances of the death to understanding (and remembering) who they were in life.

"One of the most important healing tasks for suicide loss survivors is to develop a 'bearable' narrative of the suicide."[44]

—John R. Jordan, psychiatrist

Seeking Outside Help

Many grievers of suicide seek the many forms of in-person and online help that is available. Suicide survivor groups allow for those who have experienced suicide to gather together and share stories of their loved ones. These groups include people who

Remember Them with Love

Lori says it took years to stop going over the way her father died and to remember who he was—funny, a great cook, an interesting man with interesting ideas:

> After my father's suicide, a friend's husband killed himself. I told his children that someday you will have a lot of memories of your dad and he will stop being defined as the dad who killed himself. You will start remembering him as your dad—because there are so many things he was. It's important to make sure I do that also—my father was so much more than the way he died.

Lori, interview with the author, April 2, 2022.

Suicide survivor groups provide a safe place for sharing feelings and stories with others who have experienced the trauma of suicide.

have recently experienced suicide and people who experienced it years earlier. This mixture means that people help one another at different stages of the process. Other support groups can be found through churches, synagogues, and mosques. Some offer nondenominational groups for all who grieve. Many people also find it helpful to talk with a therapist one-on-one about all of the feelings of grief and trauma resulting from suicide.

Post-Traumatic Growth After Suicide Death

In the years after a suicide death of a close friend or family member, most people find a pathway to begin to live a meaningful life again. Psychiatrist Richard Tedeschi has noticed similarities in the ways people grieve and come back from traumatic events, including suicide. He calls this process post-traumatic growth. He describes it as "the positive changes that occur in the aftermath of a trauma as a result of the process of a struggle with these traumatic events."[45] He has identified common areas in which people experience growth: increased personal strength, increased connection with and compassion toward others, greater appreciation and gratitude for their life, and engaging with questions about the purpose, meaning, and value of their life.

> "People who are resilient don't grow in the aftermath of a certain event, because they don't need to grow—they're resilient to it."[46]
>
> —Richard Tedeschi, psychiatrist

Tedeschi's definition of trauma is an event that shatters a person's core beliefs. People who experience a suicide death often lose any connection to those beliefs. I remember feeling, how could I return to the life I led? I was a mother of two children, I had an interesting job, I supported myself, and I visited my children. I thought of myself as a fairly competent mother who gave cogent advice to her children. All of that was gone. Tedeschi believes there is a difference between post-traumatic growth and resilience. Resilience suggests that individuals can bounce back and return to the way they were before, whereas people who experience trauma feel that life is over. "People who are resilient don't grow in the aftermath of a certain event, because they don't need to grow—they're resilient to it,"[46] Tedeschi says.

Keeping Memories Alive

Brit has lost several people to suicide—an uncle, a cousin, and most recently, a dear friend. The loss of her friend was especially hard, she says, because Brit is a therapist at a middle school. In her job, she often hears from students who are feeling suicidal. She felt guilty that she had not seen the warning signs in her friend. She says that she keeps these people's memories with her and that it informs her present:

> I keep things with me that each of them gave me, like talismans. I have a ring from my cousin, a flower pot from my friend. I hear their voices in my head—sometimes they say funny things, sometimes just a comment. I remember to hold on to each moment when I am with the people I love. All these moments really matter. As I get older, I realize that I have less time. I hold my husband Liam close, I know I have a partner that I love and we have a good life. I honor and respect that I am privileged to have such a life. I live my life more in the present because of the people that chose not to be here.

Brit, interview with the author, April 1, 2022.

There are many examples of post-traumatic growth among suicide survivors. Some have started foundations or talk and give lectures to suicide support groups, while others vow never to forget their deceased love one. Mike remembers, "My wife and I made a vow, the day we found our son, that we would always speak of his death. We would never shy away from telling people if they asked what had happened to him and how no one should take for granted that their child is not in danger. We wanted to memorialize Seb's story, to tell the truth about our son."[47]

Jill says that the death of her brother transformed her parenting. "People would offer advice about what I should and shouldn't do with my kids. I didn't listen and I didn't care. I did all the things others told me not to do: I held them too much. I listened to them too much. I did whatever they needed me to do whenever they needed me to do it. That is how I honor my brother's death."[48]

Gaining Understanding

The experience of deep grief allows for a kind of opening up to an understanding that other people are suffering. I definitely changed many of the ways I had of dealing with others. For one, I stopped offering advice. After all, I couldn't keep my son alive. Who was I to offer parental advice, or any other advice for that matter? I used to talk more than I listened. After the suicide, I did more listening. Finally, I found a deep compassion for others that I didn't have before.

Others describe a deep need to honor the deceased by doing something positive in the world to commemorate that person. Natalie Levy describes her journey seven months after her mother killed herself:

> Seven months later, I am here in Denver, launching a women's health and empowerment business, in many ways inspired by mom. I feel grateful to have had the time with her that I did. Now I hope to build community and give back to others the way she always did. She would light up with passion describing her work on campaign initiatives

for various community leaders, or the expressions of kids who attended music initiatives at the University of Michigan, where she helped arrange buses to transport them from inner city schools.

As I reflect upon this journey, which I am only partly through, there are still days when I am haunted by the loss, the suddenness of it, the what ifs, and my feelings of guilt and remorse. I have days when I still can't catch my breath, or have a hard time getting out of bed.

But more and more, I am able to catch my breath. To push forward, to be deliberate in my actions, and to try to be mindful of all I have. I have more happy days than sad days. When I have a down, because grief is a rollercoaster, I know it is temporary.[49]

Seeking a Return to Normal Life

While many people find a way to come to terms with a suicide loss, it is important to remember that there are many who struggle and may never be able to live a productive life. People who experience a suicide death may have feelings of harming them-

Many people struggle for the rest of their lives with a suicide loss. But others find ways to come to terms with that loss—and to once again feel happiness and do the things they love.

selves, quit their jobs, and isolate themselves from friends and family. This is especially true for people who have a difficult time bonding with others, making friends, and reaching out and talking about their emotions.

In the 2020 movie *Nomadland*, many of the characters had experienced trauma of one kind or another and dropped out to roam the country in their cars. One of the people in the movie, Bob Wells, was not an actor; he was a real-life nomad who had lost his son to suicide, and his wife had died. After revealing that his son took his life three years before, he says:

> I can still barely say that in a sentence and for a long time the question was, how can I be alive on this earth when he's not? And I didn't have an answer. And those were some hard, hard days. But, I realize that I could help him by helping people, and serving people. It gives me a reason to go through each day. Some days, its all I got . . . there are many people out here who have never gotten over their grief. And that's okay.[50]

Wells gives voice to the many for whom returning to a normal life after suicide seems next to impossible. When asked about the movie, Wells says, "I thought it was very, very true to nomadic living. They caught it completely. It's dark, because grief is dark. Becoming a nomad is about, for many of us, going through the darkness of the tunnel, looking for the light at the other end."[51]

For all who experience a suicide death, the grief does not go away. One does not get over it. But as social worker Sharon Walker puts it, "It's not that the grief gets smaller, but you grow big enough around it to start being able to manage it. . . . And then you can take it off the shelf and touch it when you want. It becomes something that you can eventually manage and live with and incorporate in your life. But as far as ever getting over it, there is no such thing."[52]

epilogue

My Personal Journey

I went from not knowing how to survive my son's death to slowly building purpose and recovering a sense of self. My job as an editor and writer was impossible. Without an ability to concentrate, reading became an exercise in futility. I had a particularly difficult client at the time, and dealing with that person became impossible. The least little bit of conflict felt painful, as though a bandage was being ripped off charred skin. I simply dropped out of society. Friends helped cover the project I was working on while I fell apart. I understood how people could simply walk away from their life. After all, something momentous had happened. I could not return to life as though it had not.

My yoga practice and yoga teachers offered me ways to cope. They encouraged me to help in yoga therapy—helping others might relieve some of the grief, they thought. They were right. Though I felt overwhelmed, I learned new skills and began helping other people. My grief made me sensitive to the other people's pain. As I learned the techniques to help people with their knee, back, or shoulder pain, I gradually came out of my own pain. Helping others allowed me to take a step toward healing.

Three years into my own grief, a dear friend's son killed himself. I rushed to her house. I held her in my arms and we both wept. I went there often, and we had long talks about God, the nature of suicide, and other conversations from the heart. I began to realize that I was far enough into my own journey of grief that I could support someone else in theirs. It was the first time that I realized I had actually started to move from a half death to a life.

Today, I still cry for my son. I still take solace in people talking about him and who he was. And I know he would want me to make sense of his death in a way that can help other people. He was like that.

If you are grieving after a suicide, know that all your feelings are normal. Falling apart one minute, not falling apart the next, it's all okay. And help is all around you. Talk about the person to someone you trust. Talk to the dead person too. Tell them everything. Most of all, please, take care of yourself. Keep one foot in front of the other and enter the life you never thought you could live. Be kind to yourself. You can never be replaced, and what you learn from this journey will be of use to others. You can be sure of that.

source notes

Chapter One:
When Someone You Know Dies from Suicide: How Can It Be?

1. Mike, interview with the author, March 2022.
2. Brett, interview with the author, March 16, 2022.
3. Mike, interview.
4. Quoted in Stacey Freedenthal, "Unwritten Goodbyes: When There Is No Suicide Note," Speaking of Suicide, April 23, 2014. www.speakingofsuicide.com.
5. Jen, interview with the author, June 2021.
6. Bill, interview with the author, November 13, 2021.
7. Quoted in Mood Treatment Center, "Left Behind After Suicide," 2021. www.moodtreatmentcenter.com.
8. Mike, interview.
9. Melissa (pseudonym), interview with the author March 7, 2022.
10. Anonymous, interview with the author, May 21, 2021.
11. Lawrence, interview with the author, June 2017.

Chapter Two:
Searching for Answers: What Happened?

12. Quoted in Checkup Newsroom, "In Their Own Words: Three Parents Open Up About Losing a Child to Suicide," May 10, 2021. www.checkupnewsroom.com.
13. Quoted in Checkup Newsroom, "In Their Own Words."
14. Yuri Battaglia et al., "The Use of Demoralization Scale in Italian Kidney Transplant Recipients," *Journal of Clinical Medicine*, July 9, 2020. www.ncbi.nlm.nih.gov.
15. Quoted in Rheana Murray, "What Is It Like to Survive a Suicide Attempt?," *Today*, September 23, 2019. www.today.com.
16. Quoted in Murray, "What Is It Like to Survive a Suicide Attempt?"
17. Sam Fiorella, "A Letter to Parents Surviving a Child's Suicide," Friendship Bench, December 2, 2015. https://thefriendshipbench.org.
18. Quoted in Murray, "What Is It Like to Survive a Suicide Attempt?"
19. Doris A. Fuller, "My Daughter, Who Lost Her Battle with Mental Illness, Is Still the Bravest Person I Know," *Washington Post*, April 20, 2015. www.washingtonpost.com.

Chapter Three:
Survivors in the Aftermath of Suicide: What Is Happening to Me?

20. Quoted in Lindsey Phillips, "Untangling Trauma and Grief After Loss," *Counseling Today*, May 4, 2021. https://ct.counseling.org.
21. Scott, interview with the author, June 2021.
22. Jen, interview.
23. John R. Jordan, "Lessons Learned: Forty Years of Clinical Work with Suicide Loss Survivors," *Frontiers in Psychology*, April 29, 2020. www.frontiersin.org.
24. Jenny Teo, "Losing My Only Child to Suicide," *My Mental Health,* November 18, 2020. https://stayprepared.sg/mymentalhealth/articles/losing-my-only-child-to-suicide
25. Marilyn, interview with the author, August 2021.
26. Quoted in Julie Halpert, "We Lost Our Son to Suicide. Here's How We Survived," *New York Times*, January 30, 2020. www.nytimes.com.
27. Marilyn, interview.
28. Lori, interview with the author, April 2, 2022.
29. Mike, interview.
30. Mike, interview.

Chapter Four:
How to Talk to Someone Who Has Experienced a Loss from Suicide

31. Jill, interview with the author, February 20, 2022.
32. Alexandra Pitman, "The Stigma Associated with Bereavement by Suicide and Other Sudden Deaths: A Qualitative Interview Study," *Social Science & Medicine*, February 2018. www.ncbi.nlm.nih.gov.
33. Quoted in Valeriya Azorina et al., "The Perceived Impact of Suicide Bereavement on Specific Interpersonal Relationships: A Qualitative Study of Survey Data," *International Journal of Environmental Research and Public Health*, May 21, 2019. www.ncbi.nlm.nih.gov.
34. Mara, interview with the author, December 20, 2021.
35. Jen, interview.
36. Melissa, interview.
37. Gayle Brandeis, "What to Say (and Not to Say) to Someone Grieving a Suicide," *New York Times*, May 8, 2019. www.nytimes.com.
38. Quoted in Pittsburgh Theological Seminary, "Praying with People Grieving Loss from Suicide," August 30, 2018. www.pts.edu.
39. Jen, interview.
40. University of Texas at Austin Counseling and Mental Health Center, "Helping a Friend Who Has Lost a Loved One to Suicide," 2021. https://cmhc.utexas.edu.

Chapter Five:
Coming Out the Other Side: Moving from Survival to Living Again

41. Andrea (pseudonym), interview with the author, February 15, 2022.
42. Mara, interview.
43. Jen, interview.
44. Jordan, “Lessons Learned.”
45. Quoted in Moya Sarner, “Post-Traumatic Growth: The Woman Who Learned to Live a Profoundly Good Life After Loss,” *The Guardian* (Manchester, UK), May 11, 2021. www.theguardian.com.
46. Quoted in Sarner, “Post-Traumatic Growth.”
47. Mike, interview.
48. Jill, interview.
49. Natalie Levy, “Post Traumatic Growth,” Medium, July 16, 2019. https://natalielevy.medium.com.
50. Bob Wells, *I Don’t Ever Say a Final Goodbye. I Always Just Say, I’ll See You Down the Road*, YouTube, April 27, 2021. www.youtube.com/watch?v=cNWonqk-TOE.
51. Quoted in *Vulture*, “Real-Life Nomad Bob Wells Poured His Own Grief into *Nomadland*,” February 24, 2021. www.vulture.com.
52. Quoted in Checkup Newsroom, “In Their Own Words.”

Alliance of Hope for Suicide Loss Survivors
www.allianceofhope.org
This organization for survivors of suicide loss provides information sheets, a blog, and a community forum through which survivors can share with each other.

American Association of Suicidology (AAS)
https://suicidology.org
The membership of AAS includes mental health and public health professionals, researchers, suicide prevention and crisis intervention centers, school districts, crisis center volunteers, survivors of suicide loss, attempt survivors, and a variety of laypersons who have an interest in suicide prevention. Its mission is to promote the understanding and prevention of suicide and support those who have been affected by it.

Friends for Survival
www.friendsforsurvival.org
Toll-free Suicide Loss Helpline: (800) 646-7322
This organization is for suicide loss survivors and professionals who work with them. It produces a monthly newsletter and runs the Suicide Loss Helpline. It also published *Pathways to Purpose & Hope*, a guide to building a community-based suicide survivor support program.

HEARTBEAT
http://heartbeatsurvivorsaftersuicide.org
This organization has chapters providing support groups for survivors of suicide loss in Colorado and elsewhere. Its website provides information sheets for survivors and a leader's guide on how to start a new chapter of HEARTBEAT.

National Alliance for Children's Grief (NACG)
https://childrengrieve.org
The NACG is a nonprofit organization that raises awareness about the needs of children and teens who are grieving a death and provides education and resources for anyone who supports them. Through the collective voice of members and partners, the organization educates, advocates, and raises awareness about childhood bereavement.

National Suicide Prevention Lifeline
https://suicidepreventionlifeline.org
24/7 Lifeline: (800) 273-8255
The National Suicide Prevention Lifeline is a national network of local crisis centers. It operates twenty-four hours a day, seven days a week, and provides free and confidential support for people experiencing a suicidal crisis or emotional distress.

Suicide Awareness Voices of Education (SAVE)
https://save.org
Founded by a mother who lost her daughter to suicide in 1979, SAVE's mission is to help prevent suicide through public awareness and education, reduce the stigma of suicidal ideation, and serve as a resource to those touched by suicide. The website provides resources, training kits, ways to get involved and donate, and more.

Survivors of Suicide Loss (SOSL)
www.soslsd.org
SOSL reaches out and supports people who have lost a loved one to suicide. Its goal is to give suicide survivors a place where they can be comfortable expressing themselves and find support, comfort, resources, and hope in a judgment-free setting.

United Suicide Survivors International
https://unitesurvivors.org
This organization is a place where people who have experienced suicide loss, suicide attempts, and suicidal thoughts and feelings and their friends and families can connect to use their lived experience to advocate for policy, systems, and cultural change. The site has many videos with suicide survivors and others.

for further research

Books

Beryl Glover, *The Empty Chair: The Journey of Grief After Suicide*. Oklahoma City, OK: In Sight, 2000.

Marilyn E. Gootman, *When a Friend Dies: A Book for Teens About Grieving & Healing*. Minneapolis, MN: Free Spirit, 2019.

Albert Y. Hsu, *Grieving a Suicide: A Loved One's Search for Comfort, Answers, and Hope*. Downers Grove, IL: InterVarsity, 2018.

Jennifer Landau, *Teens Talk About Suicide, Death, and Grieving*. New York: Rosen, 2017.

Gary Roe, *Teen Grief: Caring for the Grieving Teenage Heart*. Wellborn, TX: Healing Resources, 2017.

Internet Sources

American Psychological Association, "Coping After Suicide Loss," October 25, 2019. www.apa.org.

Gayle Brandeis, "What to Say (and Not to Say) to Someone Grieving a Suicide," *New York Times*, May 8, 2019. www.nytimes.com.

Checkup Newsroom, "In Their Own Words: Three Parents Open Up About Losing a Child to Suicide," May 10, 2021. www.checkupnewsroom.com.

Julie Halpert, "We Lost Our Son to Suicide. Here's How We Survived," *New York Times*, January 30, 2020. www.nytimes.com.

Hospice of Cincinnati, "When Someone You Love Dies by Suicide: 6 Things You Need to Know," April 3, 2019. www.cincinnati.com.

Hospital and Health Care, "Suicide Victims Often Hide Suicidal Thoughts: Study," February 19, 2019. www.hospitalhealth.com.au.

Katie Hurley, "A Guide to Working Through the Grief After a Loss by Suicide," Everyday Health, May 7, 2019. www.everydayhealth.com.

index

about the author

Bonnie Szumski is a writer and editor who lives in Encinitas, California. She has written well over fifty books and edited many more.

A personal note from Bonnie Szumski

When I lost my son, Ezekiel Steffens, to suicide in 2014 after a short and devastating bout of mental illness, I began a lifelong journey to attempt to live my life in a meaningful way. I carry my son's memory with me every single moment of every single day. The grief never goes away. On some days, I cannot even tell you that I feel it less. But I can tell you that your life and your story is meaningful. You matter, and the person you lost to suicide matters. Tell his or her story. Remember them with love. You may be angry or so sad you cannot cope sometimes. All of that is okay. But at some point, try to come to a place of renewed love. They faced pain they couldn't or wouldn't reveal, and it is not your fault. It is hard when you are facing life's struggles to see that you are loved and have a purpose that is yet to be fulfilled. Know that, without any doubt, you are deeply loved and that you can never be replaced.